To Linda, with
love and gratitude.
Thank you for a great
retreat.   Sally

2004

THE INTERVIEW WITH

GOD

All of the beautiful landscape photographs featured in The Interview With God are used with permission, under license, from the following photographers and agencies:

Photography by Larry Carver, Ron Dahlquist, Larry Dunmire, Getty Images, Steven Holt, Paul Kuroda, Greg Martin, Larry Prosor, SuperStock and Steve Vidler.

ISBN 0-9725076-6-3

Printed in the United States of America

Book created and edited by Morgan Westerman. The Interview With God poem's author is unknown.

Cover & Interior Design by JUDDesign.

get
inspired now!™
incorporated

4130 La Jolla Village Drive
Suite 107-64, La Jolla, CA 92037
www.getinspirednow.com

A NOTE ABOUT THE BOOK

The Interview With God has become a spiritual phenomenon, touching literally millions of lives around the world. The subtle reminder of a caring God is inspiring people of all walks of life and of all faiths to know that God is with us... always.

The spirit of God's love truly brings meaning and hope—what our world needs, and now receives with open arms.

Millions more are waiting for this simple and powerful message of inspiration. Our hope is that this little book will help you too, feel a little closer to heaven.

I dreamed I had an

Interview with God.

"SO YOU WOULD LIKE TO
INTERVIEW ME?"

God asked

"IF YOU HAVE THE TIME," I SAID.

GOD smiled.

"My time is eternity."

"WHAT QUESTIONS DO YOU HAVE IN MIND FOR ME?"

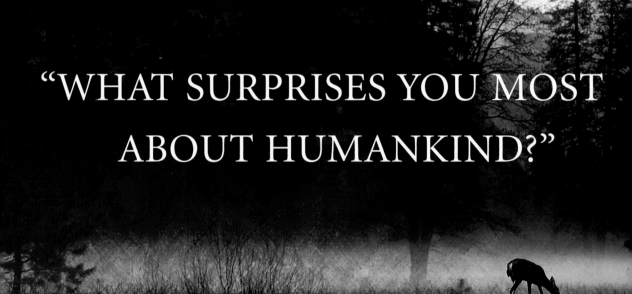

"WHAT SURPRISES YOU MOST ABOUT HUMANKIND?"

GOD
ANSWERED...

"That they get bored with

childhood,

they rush to grow up,

and then long to be

children again,"

"That they lose their health
to make money...

and then lose their money
to restore their health."

"That by thinking anxiously about the future, they **forget the present,** such that they live in neither the present **nor the future.**"

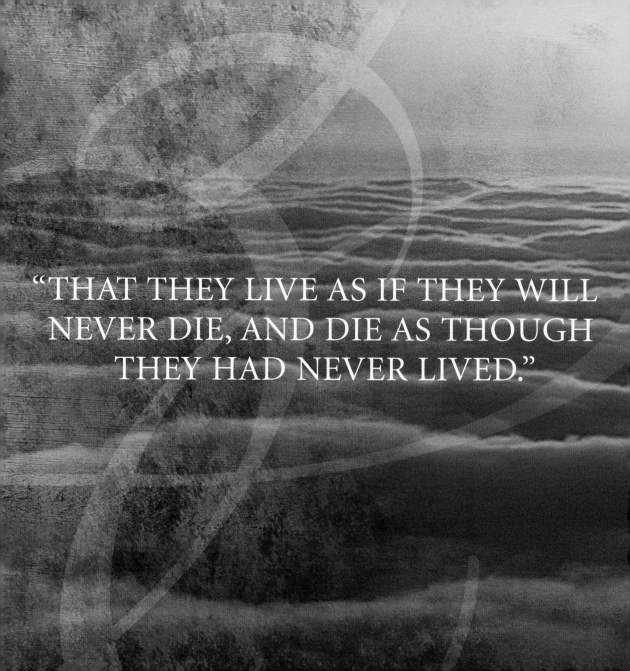

"THAT THEY LIVE AS IF THEY WILL NEVER DIE, AND DIE AS THOUGH THEY HAD NEVER LIVED."

GOD'S HAND TOOK MINE

AND WE WERE SILENT
       FOR A WHILE.

AND THEN I ASKED…

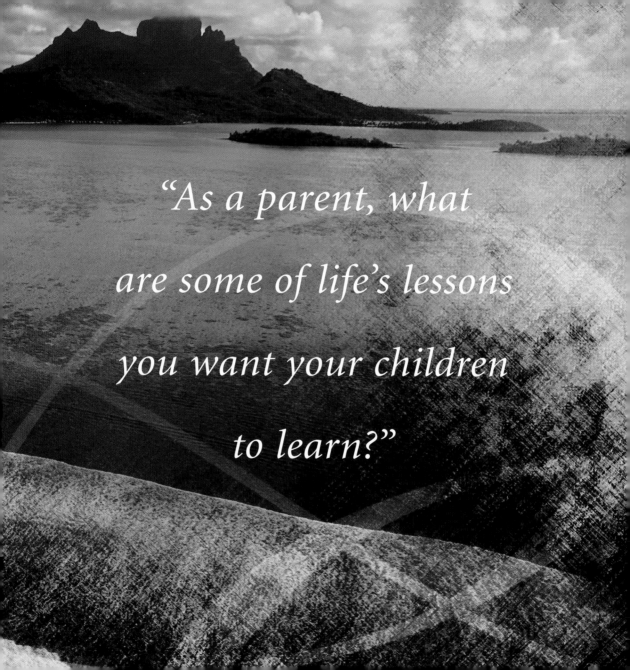

"As a parent, what are some of life's lessons you want your children to learn?"

"TO LEARN
THEY CANNOT MAKE
ANYONE LOVE THEM.

ALL THEY CAN DO IS
LET THEMSELVES

BE LOVED."

"To learn that it is not good to compare themselves

to others."

"To learn to forgive by PRACTICING FORGIV

ENESS.”

"**TO LEARN** that it only takes a few seconds to open profound wounds in those **THEY LOVE,** and it can take many years to **HEAL THEM.**"

"To learn that a rich person is not one who has the most, but is one who needs the least."

"TO LEARN THAT THERE

ARE PEOPLE WHO

LOVE THEM DEARLY, BUT

SIMPLY HAVE NOT YET

LEARNED HOW TO EXPRESS

OR SHOW THEIR FEELINGS."

LEARNED

"TO LEARN THAT TWO

AT THE SAME THING AND

PEOPLE CAN LOOK

SEE IT DIFFERENTLY."

"To learn that it is not enough that they forgive one another, but they must also **forgive themselves**."

"THANK YOU FOR YOUR TIME," I SAID HUMBLY. "IS THERE ANYTHING ELSE YOU WOULD LIKE YOUR CHILDREN TO KNOW?"

GOD
SMILED
AND SAID...

"JUST KNOW THAT I AM HERE...

always."

—AUTHOR UNKNOWN

I dreamed I had an interview

"So you would like to interview me?" God asked.

"If you have the time," I said.

God smiled. "My time is eternity."

"What questions do you have in mind for me?"
"What surprises you most about humankind?"

God answered...

"That they get bored with childhood, they rush to grow up, and then long to be children again,"

"That they lose their health to make money... and then lose their money to restore their health."

"That by thinking anxiously about the future, they forget the present, such that they live in neither the present nor the future."

"That they live as if they will never die, and die as though they had never lived."

God's hand took mine and we were silent for a while.

And then I asked...

"As a parent, what are some of life's lessons you want your children to learn?"

with GOD

God answered…

"To learn they cannot make anyone love them.
All they can do is let themselves be loved."

"To learn that it is not good to compare
themselves to others."

"To learn to forgive by practicing forgiveness."

"To learn that it only takes a few seconds
to open profound wounds in those they love,
and it can take many years to heal them."

"To learn that a rich person is not one who has
the most, but is one who needs the least."

"To learn that there are people who love them dearly,
but simply have not yet learned how to express or
show their feelings."

"To learn that two people can look at the same thing
and see it differently."

"To learn that it is not enough that they forgive one
another, but they must also forgive themselves."

"Thank you for your time," I said humbly.

"Is there anything else you would like your children
to know?"

GOD smiled and said,

"Just know that I am here… always."

— Author unknown —

"So do not fear, for I am with you;

do not be dismayed, for I am your God.

I will strengthen you and help you;

I will uphold you."

Isaiah 41:10 NIV

HAVE YOU SEEN THE ONLINE PRESENTATION YET?

Tens of millions of visitors
have been inspired by
The Interview With God
Online Presentation.

Isn't it time for you to
Get Inspired Now?
Be part of the phenomenon!
Visit www.getinspirednow.com.

ABOUT THE GET INSPIRED NOW SERIES

The Interview With God is part of the breakthrough Get Inspired Now series which includes *Pathways to Peace,* and other beloved messages. For more inspiration, visit www.getinspirednow.com.

At our website you can join our free *Get Inspired Now Newsletter,* and send free e-cards from The Interview With God. Popular gift items from The Interview With God, such as Screensavers, Greeting Cards, Journals, and more are available online at www.getinspirednow.com.

Quantity discounts for this book are available for your church or organization.

Contact us at:

Get Inspired Now!
4130 La Jolla Village Drive
Suite 107-64
La Jolla, California USA 92037

info@getinspirednow.com
1.800.813.5489

get inspired now!
inspiring millions, one soul at a time

o you would like to interview me?" God
smiled. "My time is eternity. What ques...
...prises you most about humankind?"
...ildhood, they rush to grow up, and the...
...eir health to make money... and then t...
...thinking anxiously about the future,...
...e in neither the present nor the futur...
...d die as if they had never lived." God's...
...hile. And then I asked... "As a parent,...
...ur children to learn?" "To learn they c...
...n do is let themselves be loved. To learn...
...others. To learn to forgive by practicing...
...seconds to open profound wounds in t...
...heal them. To learn that a rich person...
...eds the least. To learn that there are...
...ve not yet learned how to express or s...
...n look at the same thing and see it dif...
...at they forgive one another, but they...
...r your time... and humbly. "Is there a...
...row?" God smiled and said, "Just know...
...ke to interview me?" God asked. "If you...
...eternity. What questions do you have...
...out humankind?" God answered... "Tha...
...row up, and then long to be children...